ALL about ANTWERP

This book has been made possible with the generous co-operation
of Piet Kimzeke, cityguide in Antwerp.
Translated by Patricia Bennett.

Copyright of this publication for photographs and text:
© EDITORIAL ESCUDO DE ORO, S.A. - Palaudarias, 26 - 08004 Barcelona
VAN MIEGHEM A. n.v. Marconistraat 5, 8400 Oostende

5th Edition

I.S.B.N. 84-378-1410-3

Dep. Legal B. 521-1998

SALE DISTRIBUTOR : Editions A.V.M. n.v.
Marconistraat 5 (Industriepark) B-8400 OOSTENDE
Tel.: (059) 70.86.22 - Fax.: (059) 70.10.53

Impreso en España - Printed in Spain
FISA - ESCUDO DE ORO, S.A. - Palaudarias, 26 - Barcelona (Spain)

Introduction

Whoever visits Antwerp for the first time is astonished at the rich variety of the places of interest that the city offers. There is much to see and experience, in the sphere of both art history and commerce.

The city can be characterized in the following ways:
- as a commercial city and port with international reputation,
- as a city of art and culture where, among others, P.P.Rubens played a leading part,
- as a matchless and world-renowned centre for the diamond industry.

The art treasures in numerous museums, churches, patrician houses and historical buildings reflect a rich historical past. The port hums with intense activity and the skill of the diamond cutters is represented in the "Antwerp cut".

Judged by the number of inhabitants - half a million - Antwerp does not count among the great cities of the world, but, with the port which extends to the Dutch border, its extent is greater than that of the Belgian capital, Brussels.

It is hoped that this album of coloured photographs will enable you to remember Antwerp and also be your guide for future visits.

The Brabo fountain and the top of the Cathedral spire

Concice historical outline

The history of Antwerp began in the 2nd century of our era, but although recent excavations have established the existence of a Gallic-Romano settlement, it is not until the 10th century that Antwerp became an important city.

However, before the 10th century history was made here. In the 7th and 8th centuries christianity was preached by Saints Eligius, Amandus and Willibrord and we know that a wooden fortification was built on the "Aanwerp" of the Scheldt (a mound of silt from which the name "Antwerp" originated) and that the Norsemen destroyed this "castle" in 836.

The city was granted munipal rights in the 12th century. In the 13th it enjoyed its first period of great prosperity. This came to an halt in the years 1357-1405, since Louis of Male, Count of Flanders, incorporated Antwerp into Flanders and conferred more privileges on Bruges.

The greatest period of prosperity began in the 16th century, when Antwerp superseded Bruges as one of the most important economic and financial centres in Western Europe. Naturally many foreign merchants settled in this trading melting pot, - "Antverpia Mercatorum Emporium". Simultaneously with economic development, cultural and artistic life propered and craftmanship flourished. Under the influence of Christophel Plantin and his successors, the Moretus family, famous painters, including Albrecht Dürer, were at work here, and Quinten Metsys can be claimed as the founder of the Anwerp School of Painting .

Antwerp became a centre of cosmopolitan humanism. Erasmus and Thomas More frequently met in the home of the Antwerp recorder and humanist, Peter Giles. Since the "Golden Age" of the 16th century the inhabitants of Antwerp enjoyed in being called "Sinjoren". They acquired this title when they fancied themselves as the descendants of the senores, the Spanish overlords.

At the end of the 16th century the religious disturbances, - which set Roman Catholics and Protestants against oneanother throughout Western Europe -, had a very adverse effect on Antwerp. The year 1585 marked the end of the period of economic prosperity. The northern provinces had freed themselves from Spain. The Scheldt was closed to navigation. The population, which had risen to more than 100.000 inhabitants, dropped to about 42.000 . The wealthy merchants, together with the craftsmen and artists, sought refuge in the north.

Yet there was a revival of art in the following century with the Counter-Reformation. The tone was set by P.P.Rubens, already internationally famous as the court painter of the Spanish governors, and a number of other Antwerp painters, whose fame also had spread abroad.

The Spanish government was followed by that of Austria, and then, by the end of the 18th century, French armies were occupying the Netherlands in the north and south.

The river Scheldt was open again . Napoleon visited Antwerp and wanted to use its favourable position as a base from which to conquer England. He described Antwerp as "the pistol leveled at the heart of England", and instigated the construction of docks and shipbuilding yards

After a short period of union with the Netherlands, from 1815 to 1830, the Scheldt was again closed. Only after 1863, with the purchase of the Scheldt toll, the harbour developed unexpected opportunities. The wharves serving the centre of the city were restored in 1885, and then in the course of the 20th century the harbour has been extended in stages, as far as the Dutch frontier and on the left bank, behind great locks, the most recent of which is the largest in the world.

The harbour of Antwerp is today a distribution centre

← *The Grote Markt with a view of the Cathedral*   *The Grote Markt with guildhouses and theBrabo fountain*

of world renown for speed and efficiency. Diamond cutting and the trade in diamonds, whose foundations were laid in the 16th century, is enjoying an unexpected prosperity and with four diamond exchanges Antwerp is parapount in the diamond trade on a world scale.

The international prestige of Antwerp has manifested itself in various ways in the past: there have been three world exhibitions (in 1885, 1894 and 1930) and in 1920 the 7th Olympic Games were held here.

In 1993 Antwerp will become the "Cultural Capital of Europe", a tittle that she will hold for one year. Antwerp is a city that cherishes a tradition of tolerance and hospitality.

A visit to Antwerp is fascinating encounter with her cultural past and her rich heritage of art. Above all visitors will enjoy the convivial atmosphere, that is a special feature of life there, and come under the spell of spirit of cosmopolitism which has never been lost.

*The Grote Markt:
the Brabo fountair
and the
central elevation
of the Town Hall*

The Grote Markt: the Town Hall and the carpet of flowers

A walk through the city

Visits to Antwerp usually begin at the market place. The town hall, which dominates the triangular market place, is known as the centrepiece of the metropolis. When this building was inaugurated in 1565 the Italian renaissance was finally introduced into the Netherlands by artists and architects, such as Hans Vredeman de Vries, Pieter Coecke van Aelst and Cornelis Floris.

On the small open space in front of the cathedral, the Handschoenmarkt or glove market, you can see the small "Well of Quinten Metsys", which used to stand in front of the old city hall. It bears the gothic text "De liefde maekte van den smidt eenen schilder" (love made the smith into an artist) and it is virtually a legend. The story relates that the artistic iron decoration was made by the Antwerp painter Quinten

The Handschoenmarkt: the Quinten Metsys well and a small statue of Brabo at the top

"Gabriël", the largest bell in the carillon

The carillon mechanism

The Groenplaats with a view of the Cathedral

Metsys when, as a young man, he was a smith. He was in love with a painter's daughter, whose father did not not consider him good enough to marry his daughter. So Quinten demonstrated his skill by painting a fly, unobserved, on the recently finished canvas by the painter, and this eventually led to a reconciliation with his future father-in-law.

The Cathedral, which took nearly two centuries to build, is the largest gothic church in the Low Countries. The enormous spire, a finely sculptured stone structure, 123 m high, was completed in 1521. The town's carillon, with 49 bronze bells, is at height

The Cathedral:
the high altar
with P.P.Rubens'
"Assumption
of our Lady"
and the wooden
choir stalls

The "Deposition from the Cross" by P.P.Rubens in the Cathedral

of 90 m. The oldest and heaviest bell is called Gabriël. This is the original bell, dating from 1459 and weighing 4.840 kg. The chief architects of Our Lady's Cathedral were Jacob van Tienen, Peter Appelmans, Herman and Domien de Waghemaekere and Rombout Keldermans. Next to the main entrance there is a monument in the form of a builder's lodge in honour of Peter Appelmans.

The church has often suffered catastrophic fires, such as those in 1434 and 1533, together with attacks by the iconoclasts in 1566 and 1581 and plundering during the French occupation from 1794 to 1800. The

main entrance, destroyed by the iconoclasts in the 16th century, was rebuilt in 1903 in neo-gothic style. "The last Judgement" is depicted in the tympanum.
The altars in the church are embellished by superb paintings by P.P.Rubens: "The Raising of the Cross", "The Deposition from he Cross", "The Assumption of Our Lady" and "The Resurrection".
A visitor to the Cathedral will be struck by the many other wonderful works of art, including the windows, the pulpit, and the choir stalls finely carved in oak.
After a visit to the Cathedral there is nearby the Melkmarkt (Milk Market) by the Blauwmoezelstraat and the Lijnwaadmarkt (Linen Market) and then a

The Hendrik Conscienceplein with the Public Library

visitor should stroll through the narrow Jezuïtenrui, which leads to the Hendrik Conscience Square.
This square can also be reached by making a turn through the Wolkstraat, and at n° 37 you can enter the courtyard of the leatherworkers. These small houses were built in 1422 for elderly members of the furriers' guild, later leather curriers and afterwards shoemakers also came to live here.

By going along the Hoofdkerkstraat, passing on the right a typical old inn, "Het Gulick" (1565), you reach the Hendrik Conscience Square.
This lovely square is dominated by the baroque facade of the Church of St. Charles Borromeo. The architects, Aguillon and Huyssens, have clearly been influenced by P.P. Rubens, but they have also been inspired by the Church of Jesus in Rome. This Jesuit Church, renowned as one of the most sumptuous in the Low Countries, reflects the spirit of the Counter-Reformation. It was built between 1615 and 1621 and the marble for the walls and columns was imported from Italy.
P.P. Rubens designed 39 ceiling paintings but when lightning struck in 1718 they were all consumed by fire. Less expensive materials were used in the re-building, but the high altar and the "Houtappelkapel" still bear witness to the past glory. The square is partly enclosed by the former convent buildings of the

The front façade of the St. Charles Borromeo Church on the Hendrik Conscienceplein.

The central aisle and high altar in the St. Charles Borromeo Church

Jesuits, which became the public library in 1879. Opposite the church there is a stuatue of Hendrik Conscience, the Flemish author "who taught his people to read".

A more complete view can be obtained of the handsome baroque tower of the Church of St. Charles Borromeo by going left from the church towards St. Kathelijnevest.
We continue towards Lange Nieuwstraat, visiting on the left the attractive St. Nicolaasplaats, with its chapel, small step gables and a pump with te statue of St. Nicolaas.

Further along the street, at no.31, is the 15th century Chapel of Burgundy , where it was claimed that the marriage of Philip the Handsome and Joanna of Castille took place. In fact, their marriage actually took place on the way to Antwerp in the town of Lier. The chapel is beautifully decorated with heraldic wall paintings.

We go on to the Church of St.James (St.Jacob) entering by the side door.
It was built between 1491 and 1656 . The most important architects were Domien and Herman de Waghemaekere and Rombout Keldermans. The

*The "Houtappel"
Chapel
in the St.Charles
Borromeo Church*

Confessionals in the St.CharlesBorromeus Church

⬆ Statue of Our Lady in the
St.Charles Borromeus Church

The "Bontwerkersplaats" on Wolstraat
⬅

The "St.-Nicolaasplaats" on Lange Nieuwstraat

architeture is gothic, but the furnishings are baroque, rococo or neo-classical in style. Fortunately the furnishings, placed in over a dozen of chapels were not stolen during the French adminstration of the city. It was here that P.P.Rubens married Helène Fourment. He is buried in a chapel in the ambulatory behind the high altar. In this chapel is a painting dating back to 1634 depicting "The Madonna in the midst of Saints". The carved oak confessionals in the ambulatory with their life size figures are the work of the famous sculptor Artus Quellin the Older.

The monumental high altar is one of the most outstanding features of St.James' Church. The statue represents St.Jacobus de Meerdere and it is the work of Artus Quellin the Younger. The rich decoration is by Willem Kerrickx. Just as important are the thirty six oak choir stalls executed by Artus Quelllin the Older and the Herry brothers.

To the west, the choir is closed by a baroque organ by Forceville dating back to 1727, richly embellished with wood carvings by Michel van der Voort the Older. As a nine-year-old boy, W. A. Mozart played this authentic Forceville organ.

The baroque pulpit with the four evangelists which

The St.James
Church:
central aisle
and choir

The St.James Church: choir stools and the high altar

stands in the central aisle is the work of Lodewijk Willemssens (1675).

We now leave the church going along St.Jacobstraat past the main entrance and front facade. Had not funds been short at the time the huge tower would have been 150 m high, 27 m higher than the Cathedral.

Our walk now takes us to Keizerstraat, where we can see on the right St.Anne's Chapel (1513), a small gothic church with a baroque entrance dating back to 1624.

No.9 Keizerstraat is an impressive building, but not open to tourists. It is a fine patrician residence, known as "Our Lady's House". Perhaps you may catch a glimps of the courtyard.

On the opposite side, nos. 10 and 12, you are welcome to glance at the burgomaster's dwelling of Nicolaas Rockox. P.P.Rubens, who carried out many commissions for him, called him "my friend and patron". Nicolaas Rockox possessed a valuable collection of paintings, antique statues, coins and

*"Rockox House: " ' t Cleyn Saleth"
that Nicolaas Rockox used as a
dining room.
Above the fire place an old copy
of a portrait of Nicolaas Rockox
by P.P.Rubens*

*Two studies of
male heads by
Anton van Dyck.*

The Inner courtyard of Rockoxhouse, the residence in Keizerstraat of Burgomaster NicolaasRockox

St. Paul's Church: north aisle with confessionals and the set of paintings "15 Mysteries of the Rosary"

furniture. Thanks to the Kredietbank this burgomaster's residence has been expertly restored and as in former times it houses a collection of works of art. There are works by P.P.Rubens, Anton van Dyck, Frans Snyders, Jan Breugel 1, Quinten Metsys and Jan Sanders van Hemessen. Fine art exhibits and valuable furniture make up this fine art collection.

Frans Snijders, a contemporary and colleague of P.P.Rubens, and famous as a painter of animals, lived next to Rocokx' house.

We turn right at the end of Keizerstraat, following the Minderbroedersrui and so reaching St.Paulusstraat, where at no.22 there is an entrance to St. Paul's Church. Should this door be closed, there is an

St.Paul's Church: the confessionals

St.-Paul's Church: the "Flagellation of Christ"

St.Paul's Church: the Altar of the Rosary

*St.Paul's Church:
the Calvary*

St.Paul's Church: left, the Altar of the Rosary with a painting by Carravagio and right, the high altar with choir stalls

entrance on the Veemarkt (Cattle market).This Dominican Church (1517-1571) is a relevation for many visitors. It has rightly been discribed as "a baroque jewel in a gothic shrine".

The marble high altar is a work by P.Verbruggen the Elder and P.Verbruggen the Younger. The choir stalls are also a fine example, in oak, of the work of Verbruggen the Elder. On the supporting columns no motif has been repeated. Next to the choir stalls, the lion gates provide another example of wood carving. The confessionals and the panelling which adorn the side aisles are unsurpassed. Figures that are nearly life-size are situated alongside each confessional, each depicting a special theme. Hundreds of cherubs, animals, flowers and plants are playfully represented on the panelling and the motif of garland is frequently seen.

On the wall of the northern side aisle an exceptional series of paintings depicts "The Fifteen Mysteries of the Rosary". Some of the great masters of the Antwerp School of Painting are represented, including P.P.Rubens, A.van Dyck, J.Jordaens and C.De Vos.

The Brewers' House Museum : the Treadmill

The church possesses three works of P.P.Rubens: "The Adoration of the Shepherds" , "The Dispute over the Blessed Sacrament" and "The Flagellation" .

Do not fail to see the Calvary (16697-1747) on the west side of the church, where life-size figures of prophets, angels, saints and pilgrims line the way to the "Garden of Jerusalem".

When we leave the church a detour via St.Paulus-straat, St.Pietersvliet and Scheldekaaien brings us to Adriaan Brouwersstraat, and the "Brouwershuis", the smallest museum in the city, but well worth a visit. Gilbert van Schoonbeke erected this building in the 16th century. He devised an ingenious system to supply sixteen surrounding breweries with fresh water.

The Brewers' House Museum:
the staircase

The Brewers' House Museum:
the Council Chamber

Butchers' Hall:
the former
guildhouse of
the butchers

Butchers' Hall:
a lower room

Butchers' Hall: the
Council Chamber

Butchers' Hall: the Retabel of Averbode

Butchers' Hall: the statue of St.George.

Butchers' Hall: a Ruckers' harpsichord.

The Spanish "poortjes" or "deurkens" (entrances) belong to the historic face of Antwerp. They mostly date from the late 16th and 17th centuries, being baroque in style.
They did not only embellish the dwellings of wealthy citizens and merchants , but are found in chapels, almhouses and monastries.

"Spaans poortje" of the House "Bolonia la Grassa" on Lange Nieuwstraat nr.45

Information about the way the system worked is available in the "rosmolen" (treadmill).The brewers used to meet in the impressive council chamber, with its golden leather hangings.

We retrace our steps, left along the Scheldekaaien, and again by way of St.Pietersvliet and St. Paulusstraat, but going further Nosestraat, and across the Veemarkt to the Vleeshouwersstraat, which leads to the imposing Vleeshuis (Butchers' Hall), built by the architects Domien and Herman de Waghemaekere, between 1501 and 1504. It is a splendid example of secular architecture. The meat market was on the ground floor and above a number of council chambers and banqueting rooms were at the disposal of the butchers.

The trade was brought to an end by the French adminstration and another use was found for the building. It became a museum for applied arts and archeology, illustrating the past of Antwerp. The collection is very varied and the world famous harpsichords of Antwerp are especially valuable. The workshop of Hans Ruckers had made Antwerp the centre of harpsichord building in Western Europe. Other very interesting exhibits include the "Retabel van Averbode" (1514), a picture in tiles, an Egyptian mummy, furniture, ceramics, glass, weapons, stone sculpture and the lapidarium.

When you leave the museum visit the restored quarter of the city which gained the "Europa Nostra" prize. Finally, by way of Braderijstraat, we return to the Grote Markt, the starting point of our long walk.

The Town Hall: the main stair case with wallpaintings remembering the "Golden Age" of Antwerp

Grote Markt with Town Hall and Brabo-fountain

Our second long walk could well be named "museum route", since along its way you will see other important museums. Before we begin, let us visit the Town Hall whose fine Renaissance facade we admired on our earlier walk.

The interior underwent many alterations in the 19th century. There was, in the 16th centrury, a courtyard in the centre, where merchants were allowed to erect shops, 45 in number. You have seen the entrance to these shops on the gabled side. The city's artillery was

also kept here, and this was one of the reasons why, in 1576, the "Spanish Fury" plundered the Town Hall and set it on fire. The strong outer walls were undamaged and restoration work under the protestant administration of Burgomaster Marnix van St. Aldegonde was quickly set in motion.

The courtyard was roofed in 1880 and the staircase up to the first floor was built. The five wallpaintings recall the "Golden Age" of Antwerp, depicting navigation, trade, music, the arts and letters.

The Coat of Arms of Antwerp is resplendent above

the gallery of the staircase and the arms of Antwerp's institutions are emblazoned on the cupola, together with wooden figures representing artisans.

Official receptions are held in the Leys Hall, named after the painter who in the last century, embellished the walls with scenes depicting the former freedoms of the city.

The wedding room, where wallpaintings represent marriage through the centuries, provides a splendid setting in which to begin conjugal life. In addition there is a gallery, the militia room and the towncouncil chamber. There are portraits of the Royal Family and on copper tablets on the walls the names of all the burgomasters from 1409 are recorded .

We leave the City Hall and go to the rear of the building where, at nos. 2-6 Gildekamersstraat, the Museum of Regional Ethnology is situated. Here there are objects relating to popular religion, medicine, every day life, popular art, and marionettes from puppet theaters, as well as an 18th century alchemist's chamber and a complete old chemists shop and drugstore. Such an

The Town hall: thebetrothal room with wall paintings depicting marriage through the ages

The Town Hall: the Council Chamber where the meetings of the Town Council are held

overall picture of Flemish folk life certainly deserves a visit.

At the corner, at Suikerrui no. 19, is the Ethnographic Museum giving as it were a window on the world. You can make a voyage of discovery in the distant past, as well as nowadays, of four continents. A collection with 2.000 objects on show at any time, and many more in reserve, provides insight into the wide variety of cultures in overseas countries, in Africa, America, Asia and the South Seas. Displayed over the five floors are art and artefacts from non-European countries: African sculpture is represented by statues from religion, magic, fortune-telling; the American exhibits extend from the Polar people of the far North and the Indians of the northern part, the pre-Columbian culture in Central and South America. An overall picture of Asia is given from Afghanistan to the Far East, whilst from the South Seas the culture of the Asmat-Papuan people occupies a prominent place.

The Ethnographic Museum on the Suikerrui

The Vlaaikensgang, an ideal place to listen the carillon concerts on Monday evenings in summer

↓

Proceeding in the direction of the Oude Koornmark we come to no.16, the entrance of the very picturesque "Vlaaikensgang", where the cathedral bell-ringers lived in former times. It is a delightful place from which to listen to carillon concerts on Monday evening in the summer.

The end of "Vlaaikensgang" is in Pelgrimstraat where we turn left, gaining a wonderful view of the slim cathedral spire.

We go right, along the Oude Koormarkt, towards Groenplaats, with the stately statue of P.P.Rubens in the middle.

Going on further we notice the small, much frequented Chapel of the Virgin's Nativity (1477), a popular oratory commonly known as the Shoemakers' Chapel.

From the Meirbrug we look at the 100 meter high "Boerentoren", built by a Boerenleenbank in 1929-1932 and now the seat in Antwerp of the Kredietbank.

The Ethnographic Museum: the second floor with exhibits relating to Buddhism and Hinduism

The Museum of Regional Ethnology: "Kermis" Organ produced in Antwerp by Th.Mortier (1902)

Groenplaats, looking towards the Cathedral

This was the first skyscraper to be built in Europe, and it was damaged in 1944 by a V-bomb. Thanks to its position at the beginning of the Meir it is a prominent feature of the city.

The Meir, the main commercial artery of Antwerp, connects the old town centre with the very busy area around the Central Station, which was developed in the end of the 19th century.

We continue along the Meir, noticing the good-humoured crowds and the shop windows. One of the four entrances of the former Commercial Exchange can be seen at the end of a narrow street to the left, the Twaalfmaandenstraat.

Do not be misled by the date of the facade that was restored in 1858 after a fire. The original building dated from 1531-1532, when it was the first great Commercial Exchange in Western Europe.

Going on past the mostly neo-classical facades of the Meir, we pass the statue of Anton van Dyck (1599-1641), the Antwerp artist whose paintings at the English royal court brought him world fame.

On the corner of the Wapper, to the right, is the former

Madonna statues are to be seen on many street corners.

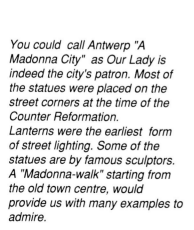

The Meir, the busiest shopping street

You could call Antwerp "A Madonna City" as Our Lady is indeed the city's patron. Most of the statues were placed on the street corners at the time of the Counter Reformation.
Lanterns were the earliest form of street lighting. Some of the statues are by famous sculptors. A "Madonna-walk" starting from the old town centre, would provide us with many examples to admire.

Royal Palace, built in 1745-1750 by the architect J.P.van Baurscheit. It was the princely residence of a merchant J.A. van Susteren. During the French Rule a bedroom in Empire style, which is still to be seen, was installed for a visit by Napoleon. The building is now used as an International Cultural Centre, where various streams of contemporary art may be seen.

On the right of the Meir, at no. 58, there is a building in classic Francis I style. Four figures at the first floor represent the evolution of lighting: the torch of prehistoric man, a roman lamp, candle light and gaslight, which over the centuries have led to modern street lighting.

Opposite at no.85 there is the elegant "Osterriethhuis" a patrician residence from the 18th century, accomplished in early rococo style by J.P.van Baurscheit Still on the right of the Meir we pass the Civic Festivity Hall and a department store, both buildings in the eclectic style dating from the beginning of this century. At the corner of Leysstraat and Jezusstraat there is a

The Meir with Anton van Dyck's statue and aview of the "Boerentoren".

The Royal Palace on the Meir

statue of Lodewijk van Berckem, apparently standing on a triumphal balcony. It is said that this famous diamond dealer from Bruges invented the art of diamond cutting. It is certainly true that he brought the diamond trade and industry from Bruges to Antwerp in the 15th century.

As is to be expected, Antwerp possesses a Diamond Museum, said to be the pearl in the crown of the museums of Antwerp. It is situated at Lange Herentalsestraat 31-33, in the heart of the diamond region, near the Central Station. You are quite near to it at the corner of the Leys- and Jezusstraat; proceed along the Leysstraat, where the buildings in "fin de siècle" style give grandiose expression to the prosperites of Antwerp at the beginning of this century. As you cross the "Leien", - known as the "Boulevard"- , look left at the sumptuous "Royal Flemish Opera House".

Nearer the Central Station the second turning on the right leads into Lange Herentalsestraat, where a visit to the Provincial Diamond Museum is a fascinating and compelling experience. Every aspect of the dia-

The "Antwerp cut" is worldfamous

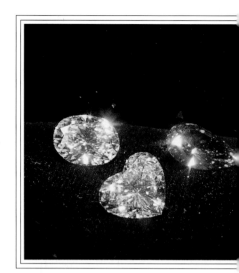

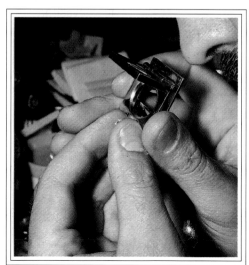

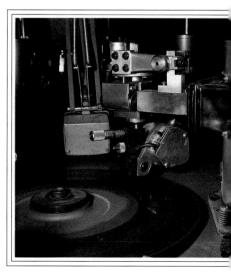

The Provincial Diamond Museum: an old diamond cutters' place

The Royal Flemish Opera House

mond industry and trade is explained and you will readily acknowledge the outstanding skill of the diamond workers of Antwerp. The "Antwerp cut" receives worldwide recognition and without exaggeration one can say that the greatest diamond trade in the world is found here. The visit ends in the treasury where you can admire a glittering display of traditional and contemporary diamond jewelry.

If you wish to make a further museum visit, retrace your steps along the De Keyserlei, Leysstraat and the Meir as far as the Wapper.
On this square, near the Meir, with its fountain and statue of an eagle (by Hugo Lisberg, 1931), the Rubens House is situated on the left at no. 9.
Peter Paul Rubens (1577-1640) married Isabella Brandt in 1609 and in 1610 he bought this site on

Rubens House: "Selfportrait" (1630) by P.P.Rubens

Facade of Rubens House on the Wapper

the Wapper and began to built a princely residence. The facade itself reveals the double source of his artistic aspiration: the Flemish roots and the Italian influence. To the left is the private house, built of brick in the local style with step gables and cruciform windows; to the right his studio shows a strong Italian influence, constructed from sandstone, as it is with rounded windows and a projecting cornice.

When we enter his house we are struck by the majestic portico in flamboyant baroque style and the perspective towards the pavillon at the end of the garden. His humanism is embodied in the range of architectural styles, with the Flemish courtyard on the one hand and on the other the facade in Italian style with decorations from antique mythology.

The portico, an original piece of architecture designed by Rubens, which is featured in some of his paintings,

connects the house and the studio and separates the courtyard from the garden.

As we pass through the house, the furniture, paintings and objects d'art evoke the atmosphere of the time of Rubens. We pass trough the parlour, the kitchen and the serving room to the dining room where Rubens' selfportrait hangs.

In the "Kunstkamer" we encounter an array of objects that Rubens kept . They include his sketches for oil paintings and of considerable historical interest, the "Kunstkamer van Cornelis van der Geest". This wealthy merchant, who commissioned Rubens to paint the famous alterpiece, the "Kruisverhefing" (Raising of the Cross), possessed a rich art collection. In his gallery famous artists were represented, including Quinten Metsys, P.P.Rubens, Albrecht Dürer and Adam Elsheimer, whose works are now dispersed among foreign art galleries. We recognise well known figures, including Archduke Albrecht and his Duchess, Isabella, Cornelis van der Geest himself, P.P. Rubens, the Burgomaster Rocokx, A. van Dyck, Frans Snijders and many other prominent citizens.

On the upper floors the other private apartments are to be found, including the large bedroom, where it is thought that Rubens died on May 30th 1640.

We pass along the tribune to the landing which affords a good view of the courtyard.

We enter the painter's studio with the respect he deserves. It was here that Rubens and his associates produced the masterpieces that are now the pride of many churches and art collections in Belgium and elsewhere. One of his earliest paintings, "Adam and Eve", is here, clearly showing the influence of his famous teacher, Otto Venius. Other works by Rubens are "De boodschap aan Maria" (The Annunciation), "De Moorse Koning" and two cherubs.

Rubens House: the dining room

Rubens House: the art gallery

Jan Wildens, a landscape artist who collaborated with Rubens, is represented by a decorative "Landscape with figures". The artist has borrowed two figures from "A shepherd embraces a sheperdess", by Rubens, which is now in the Alte Pinakotek in Munich. There is also the large canvas "Neptune and Amphitrite" by Jacob Jordaens, a mythological work that clearly shows the influence of Rubens.

We can take a well-earned rest in the garden, laid out in Italianate-Flemish style that was common in Rubens' time.

When we leave Rubens' majestic residence we go left to the end of the Wapper, where we see the rear of the modern theatre complex, where there are regular productions by the Royal Netherlands Theatre and the Royal Youth Theatre.

Each Saturday and Sunday morning the well known "Vogelmarkt" (bird market) which draws visitors from far and wide, takes place on the nearby square. Despite its name this is not a market confined to the sale of birds and live animals. Everthing that can attract costumers is offered for sale and lively demon-

*Rubens' House:
"Adam and Eve",
an early work
by P.P.Rubens*

Rubens House: the portico

Rubens House: the garden

Rubens House: the garden with pavillon

Rubens House: the courtyard and studio

strations of merchandise provide part of the charm. By going right along the Schuttershofstraat and then taking the second turning left, we reach the Komedieplaats with the Bourlaschouwburg, a late-classical building by the architect P.Bourla, dating from 1834, which formerly housed the Royal Netherlands Theatre. The monumental semi-circular facade is decorated at the top with statues of the nine muses.

Past the theatre facade we reach Leopoldstraat where we turn right into Arenbergstraat, at the end of which we turn left into Lange Gasthuisstraat, stopping in front of no. 33, the "Maagdenhuis".

This historical building formed part of a complex called "Elzenveld", whose history goes back to the beginning of the 13th century when Our Lady's Hospital, later called St.Elisabeth's Hospital, was established here.

In an adjacent house, the residence of the 16th century Burgomaster Marnix van Sint-Aldegonde, you find the headquarters of the Openbaar Centrum voor Maatschappelijk Welzijn (the Public Centre for Social Welfare). This organization has restored to great effect some of the hospital wards, a former cloister, priest's house and chapel, converting them into a

Komedieplaats. Bourla Theatre

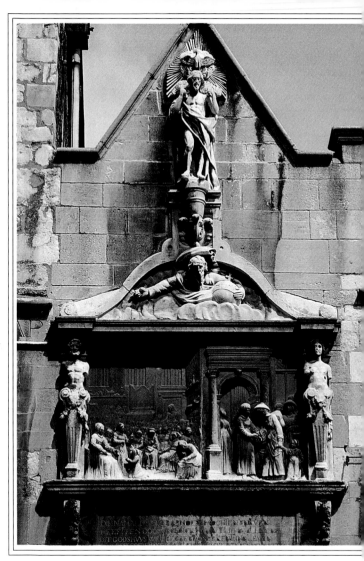

Maagdenhuis : the facade

Maagdenhuis: a bas-relief above the entrance

social-cultural centre with congress facilities. The hospital has a modern extension. There is a good collection of pictures in the "Maagdenhuis", including works by P.P.Rubens, A.van Dyck, J.Jordaens ans O.Venius, as well as furniture and objects d'art.

It is a good idea to begin a visit to the whole complex in the centuries' old botanical garden, situated on Leopoldstraat.

Retracing our steps we now visit the Mayer van den Bergh Museum at no.19, a house with a neo-gothic facade. The mother of the art collector, Ridder Fritz Mayer (1858-1901), erected this house in order to display there the art treasures of her deceased son. The collection consists of more than three thousand objects: paintings, sculpture, tapestries, coins and textiles.

The visitor will be struck by the variety of the works of art. To mention but a few: there is the life sized group in walnut, gilded and polychromed in gothic style, depicting "John resting against the breast of Christ", a

The gothic Our Lady's Chapel in Elzenveld

The Elzenveld Centre offers contempory reception facilities in historic surroundings in the heart of the city.
The restored wards of the St.Elisabeth Hospital, together with the reception hall, adjacent rooms from the convent, the chaplain's house and the 15th century gothic chapel offer first class accommodation for congresses and cultural activities.

The Dr.Marquis Auditorium at "Elzenveld"

Museum Mayer van den Bergh: the interior

work from the beginning of the 14th century by Master Heinrich van Konstanz. From about 1400 there is a rare example of Dutch painting on wood, known as the "Antwerpen-Baltimore", from the Maas-Rhein region. In addition there is a masterpiece of South-Netherlands miniature painting in the form of the "Mayer van den Bergh Breviary", with illuminations by Gheeraert Horenbaut, Simon Bening and Jan Provost.
One of the finest exhibits is the "Dulle Griet"(1566) by Pieter Breugel the Elder, one of the master's most fascinating works.

We leave the museum and go right into the Korte Gasthuisstraat. At the start of this shopping street stands the statue called "Den Deugniet" , a mischievous Antwerp lad, who like "Manneke-Pis" in Brussels receives many uniforms and costumes on festival occasions from groups and visitors.

At the end of Korte Gasthuisstraat, where there is a confluence of shopping streets, called "De Wilde Zee", we go left into Lombaardvest at the end of which there is yet another museum, the Dagblad-

Mayer van den Bergh Museum:
"John resting on the breast of Jesus" (1300)

Mayer van den Bergh Museum: facade

Mayer van den Bergh Museum: 14th century glass window

Mayer van den Bergh Museum: the interior

museum (Newspaper Museum). A plaque on the walll recals that Abraham Verhoeven published the first daily paper in the world in this house in 1605. The collection contains more than 500.000 papers including special editions, like the smallest and the largest newspapers in the world.

We go now our way along Steenhouwersvest, taking the first street to the right which leads to the Fridaymarket with the Plantin Moretus Museum.
The 18th century front facade masks one of the loveliest patrician houses in Antwerp, dating from the

17th century. In 1620 the humanist Woverius of Antwerp wrote the following words about the residences of his two friends, P.P.Rubens and Balthazar Moretus: "These dwellings will astonish foreigners and enthral travellers".

Christoffel Plantin (1520-1589), who came from Tours in France, was the founder of the world famous printing press and his son-in-law and successor, Jan Moretus, extended its fame. The house remained in the possession of the Moretus family for three hundred years until, in 1876, Edward Moretus sold it,

together with its entire contents to the city of Antwerp, where it is now one of the most valuable museums. Let us enter this authentic house and work place.

We begin our visit in the "Hall of Tapisteries" and admire the fine Flemish hangings from the 16th century. The carved corbles of the ceiling beams show variations of the emblems and mottoes of Christoffel Plantin and Balthazar Moretus, in nearly every room; "Labore et Constantia" is represented by a pair of compasses (the turning compass leg symbolizes work and the fixed leg symbolizes constancy) whilst "Stella Duce" is represented by a star (the guiding star).

Ten portraits by P.P.Rubens hang in the Great Salon. Together with Balthazar Moretus, the grandson of Plantin, he had attended the school of Meester Rombaut Verdonck, and the two remained friends for life. This explains why Rubens painted so many portraits of the Moretus family, and lent his assistance to the illustration of numerous books and printed material.

Two art galleries from he 17th century are to be admired as fine examples of Antwerpian craftmanship.

After these is the "Drawings and handwriting room". To the left of the entrance, in a display case, are the chronicles of Froissart, a marvellous example of the Flemish art of illumination in the 15th century.

Mayer van den Bergh Museum:
Interieurs

The Newspaper Museum. Abraham Verhoeven printed the first daily paper in the world here in 1605

The Newspaper Museum shows more than only daily papers

Vrijdagmarkt with a statue of St.Catherina and the facade of the Plantin-Moretus Museum

Opposite is the two volume Bible of King Wenceslas of Bohemia, an impressive example of the Czechoslovakian miniaturists' skill. There are valuable examples of handwriting from the 9th to the 18th century in the show cases.

We pass through the inner court at which Balthazar Moretus is looking and going through the actual shop, designed for local trade, we reach the "Salon of Tapestries", whose walls are hung with "Oudenaardse" tapestries.

In the small room that comes next, we can study the origins and history of books.

The wooden correction table, placed by the window in the "Proof readers' room", bears the scars of many centuries' use. We now enter the oldest part of the Plantin House, that Christoffel Plantin would have known. The office is hung with golden leather from Mechlin. We go through the "Room of Justus Lipsius", hung with rare 16th century Spanish leather, the "Room of the Humanists" and the type store, and at

Plantin-Moretus Museum: the "Great Salon" with portraits by P.P.Rubens

The courtyard in the Plantin-Moretus Museum

Plantin-Moretus Museum: the letter foundry

Plantin-Moretus Museum: the proof readers' room

Plantin-Moretus: the printing shop

Plantin- Moretus: the main library

"De stirpium historiae commentariorum"
by Rembert Dodoens,
printed by Plantin in 1583.

"Rhetorium liber" (Cicero), a 15th century manuscript.

The "Biblia Regia" or "
Biblia Polyglotta",
a bible in five languages,
Christoffel Plantin' s
most important work
printed in 1568-1572.

"La magnifique et somptueuse pompe funèbre fait aux obseques et funérailles du très grand et très victorieus empereur Charles 5ème célébrées en la ville de Bruxelles", printed by Plantin in 1559.

last enter the printing works. To the left are the type boxes, waiting for the type setters and opposite, the presses of which some are in perfect working order. This is the heart of the printing works where the masterpieces were produced that brought worldwide fame to the "Officina Plantiniana".

On the first and second floors there are various examples of valuables books and printed matter, including Christoffel Plantin's most important work, the "Biblia Polyglotta" and the Gutenberg bible, which he had bought. After this there are the living rooms of the Moretus family, the original type foundry and finally, the well-stocked library.

When we leave the museum we go left, passing the "Prentenkabinet" and reach the Grote Markt by way of the Heilig Geeststraat and the Hoogstraat.

However, since you are in the Sint Andrieskwartier at the Plantin Moretus Museum, you can begin the third long walk from there.

Our third expedition starts from the Grote Markt. It is now our intention to visit the Museum of Fine Arts, looking into some other museums as well in the old southern district of the city.

At first we go along the Oude Koornmarkt, looking at "De Cluyse House", at no.2, which was given by the town government to the members of the German Hanse in 1468. They remained there until 1568 when they moved to premises in the newly constructed harbour, the "Oosterlingenhuis", that was unfortunately destroyed by fire in the last century. "De Cluyse" is remarkable for the upper part of the facade which reminds us of the wooden construction of the 15th and 16th centry gables.

We go through the narrowing Oude Koornmarkt, coming into Kammenstraat and going on into Nationalestraat, a long shoppingstreet that traverses the old Sint-Andrieskwartier.

Our aim is the St.Andriesstraat to our right, where to the left is the St.Andrieskerk (St. Andrew's Church). On the small grassy square in front of the church is a statue of "Netje", the mother in the novel "Mother, what is the point of living ?" by the Antwerp writer Lode Zielens, who described the hard life of the people in this working class district.

The course of construction of the church was, so some extent, chequered. A beginning was made in late gothic style in 1522 but the spire was not built until the 18th century. The high altar is a carved "Exaltation of the Assumption of Our Lady" (17th century by P.Verbruggen the Elder). Against the clustered column there is a statue in white marble, a fine example of the high baroque style made by Artus Quellin the Elder in 1658. Obliquely opposite, in the south transept there is a epitaph on the clustered column dating from 1620, by R. and J. de Nole. Is was erected to the memory of Mary

St.Andrew's church

65

St.Andrew's church:
interior with
St.Peter and
high altar

Queen of the Scots by two ladies of her court, Barbara Moubray and Elisabeth Curlé who found refuge in Antwerp.

Without doubt one of the most famous works of art in St.Andrew's Church is the pulpit (1821, by J.B.van Hool and J.F.van Geel). It is a lively representation of Matthew, chapter 4, verses 18-20: "Follow me and I wil make you fishers of men". In the west corner of the church is a reliquary of 36 saints, a shrine that in early times was carried in processions.

When we leave the church we can reach Nationalestraat again by way of Pompstraat and Steenbergerstraat. The local writers Lode Zielens and Hendrik Conscience lived in Pompstraat as memorial tablets proclaim.
The building at the end of Nationalestraat on the left is the Institute for Tropical Medicine, world famous for medical research.

In St.Andrew's church:
Mary Stuart's epitaph and the
famous carved pulpit

The busy Nationalestraat runs into Volksstraat where at no.40 you find the former Liberaal Volkshuis "Help yourself" (1901) with a facade in Art-Nouveau style. There are incidentally numerous houses in Antwerp in Art-Nouveau or Jugendstil, including several in the neighbouring Schildersstraat, and a whole district in the style of "belle epoch" in the Cogels-Osylei, which deserves a separate expedition.

Going on through the Volksstraat we reach the Leopold de Waelplein with the impressive Royal Museum of Fine Arts. This temple of art, built in

Royal Museum of Fine Art: staircase with representations of all artists who have worked in Antwerp

1884-1890 by the local architects J.Winders and F.Van Dijk is an example of monumental eclectic architecture. We reach the massive entrance by a broad flight of steps and go into the museum, where the collection represents local and foreign artists' work. Although painting from the 14th century to the present days is included, most of the works are by Flemish masters. Out of the profusion we only name Jan van Eyck, Rogier van der Weyden, Hans Memlinc, Quinten Metsys and Joachim Patinir.

The Antwerp School of Painting of the 16th and 17th centuries is well represented. The Rubens gallery contains twenty three of the master's paintings and canvasses by Antoon van Dyck and Jacob Jordaens hang in the adjacent rooms.

For those interested in the 19th century and modern works there are several examples. There is a large collection of works by R.Wouters, as well as works by H.Leys, J.Stobbaerts, H.De Braekeleer, J.Ensor, J. Smits, P.Delvaux and R.Margritte.

There is so much to see that a visit here takes considerable time.

The massive facade
of the
Royal Museum
of Fine Art

In the Royal Museum of Fine Art:
the gallery of Van Dyck and Jordaens.

"Mary at the fountain" (detail)
by Jan van Eyck (1375-1440)

"Skeletons disputing over a hanged man"(1891)
by James Ensor (1860-1949)

A gallery with art from the 19th and 20th centuries

*Art-Deco facade of the Museum of
Contemporary Art*

*The Museum of Contemporary Art:
restaurant with wall painting by Keith Haring*

We are now in the old southers distric of the city where World Exhibitions were held in 1885 and 1894 and where it is worthwhile making an effort to visit other museums. They are accommodated in storehouses of the former docklands. The great square near the docks is used as a car park and the annual Sinksenfoor takes place here at Whitsunt. It is not so far away from the Royal Museum of Fine Arts, you just need to walk through Verschansingstraat to the old and now transferred city gate (also called The Royal Gate, since it was built in 1624 in honour of Philips II of Spain) and on the far side of the square, housed in the former "Vlaanderen" warehouse, you will find the Provincial Museum of Photography.

*Provincial Museum of Photography
in the former "Vlaanderen" warehouse*

*Provincial Museum
of Photography:
a historic camera
used to make
ordnance maps*

*Provincial Museum
of Photography: the
"Keizerspanorama"*

This museum should not be missed. It provides a complete survey of the history of photography, with authentic exhibits ranging from camera obscura to electronic apparatus. Interesting exhibitions of photography are frequently held in the Lieven Gevaertzaal. It is no exaggeration to say that the Provincial Museum of Photography in Antwerp is one of the five best photographic museum in the world.

If you go in the direction of the city centre, you will find the Museum of Contemporary Art in Leuvenstraat in a buiding with an Art-Deco facade. The most recent creations of modern art can be seen here.

Opposite the corner of the building, on the Scheldekaaien at Hangar 15, there is the "Miniature City of Antwerp". Many of the historic buildings in the city can be seen here reproduced in miniature.

You can return to the city centre either on foot along the Scheldekaaien and over the south terrace or by public transport from Leopold de Waelplein near the Royal Museum of Fine Arts.

In the "Miniature City of Antwerp" models represent the most important historical buildings in the city.
They are the work of amateur model makers who devote hours of their free time to the task. You can see them at work.
Models that are already in place include:
  - the Town Hall
  - the Butchers' Hall
  - the Steen

Koningin Astrid Square with the Central Station and Zoo entrance

The next visit takes us in one of the main tourist attractions in Antwerp: the Zoo.

We can reach it either by walking along Groenplaats, Meir and the De Keyserlei to the Central Station or we can take the pre-metro alighting at "Diamant" near the Central Station. The Central Station, built in 1905 by the architect L.J.J.de la Censerie, in striking neo-baroque style, has an impressive appearance. We go inside for a moment to look at the entrance hall with its marble stairs and massive dome.

The Zoo entrance is on Koningin Astrid Square next to the Central Station. The Antwerp Zoo, founded in 1843, is one of the most modern and progressive in the world. One of its features is the original way in which animals from all quarters of the globe are accommodated. A number of primates are expertly housed. In the building of the exotic birds the visitor is standing in darkness, separated from the cages by a "light barrier". The "nocturama" building takes us into an unknown world where, in artificial darkness, we may observe noctural animals. A visit to the reptile house is sensational. To reach it we must pass

Scenes from the Zoological Garden

75

The De Keyserlei with the Central Station

through a jungle, where tree snakes, iguanas and birds are at large and the air is full of exotic sounds and smells. Should you also wish to visit the dolphin show, you will realize that the time is too short and that a day at the Zoo passes all too quickly.

Some distance from the centre at no.91 Belgiëlei, there is an impressive bourgeois dwelling, housing the Smidt van Gelder Museum. By public transport (pre-metro) it is not so far from Groenplaats or Central Station.

Ridder Pieter Smidt van Gelder (1878-1956) gave his residence and his art collection to the city. He collected mainly 18th century items of elegant furniture, paintings and tapistries which are displayed against a harmonious background. During the 18th century French culture set the tone in Europe and so the furniture in this collection is mostly in Louis XV and Louis XVI style. In addition the museum has a wealth of porcelain. In its show cases we can admire fine examples of the finest Sèvres porcelain, with the famous "rose Pompadour" and "blue turquoise" designs.

There is also the important collection of Chinese

Ridder Smidt van Gelder Museum.
Salon on the garden side and ...

... room with "Chinoiseries"

porcelain in famille-verte glaze, typical of the time of Emperor K'ang Hsi (1662-1722) and the "famile-rose" of "Ching" porcelain, characteristic of the time of Emperor Chien-Lung (1736-1795). Do not fail to admire the "Chine de commande" porcelain, with decoration and shapes commissioned for export to Europe. There is also porcelain from the manufacturers that radiated from Saxony at the beginning of the 18th century: Meissen, Höchst, Ludwigsburg, Frankenthal and Berlin.
Certainly this is a museum for connaisseurs.

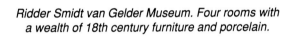

Ridder Smidt van Gelder Museum. Four rooms with a wealth of 18th century furniture and porcelain.

Statue of "Lange Wapper" (A.Poels) at the entrance of the Steen Castle. ➡

Promenade at the Steen Castle near the departure point of the "Flandria" boat trips

Whoever visits Antwerp naturally goes to the waterfront to the place of origin of the town.

The Steen Castle never fails to catch the eye. According to the Brabo legend the giant Druoon Antigoon is supposed to have lived here. However the Steen dates from the beginning of the 13th century. It was the residence of the Margrave of Antwerpen and later served as a prison.

In 1520 the Emperor Charles V completely restored it after it had fallen into decay. Its ceased to be a prison in 1823 and served various purposes prior to the establishment here of the "National Maritime Museum".

In front of the Steen stands the statue of "Lange Wapper", which is something of a joke. According to legend he lived beside the moat and took develish pleasure in suddenly turning himself into a giant, running over the roof tops in order to frighten people.

The displays in the Maritime Museum are arranged in twelve rooms and show everything connected with navigation and the fishing industry.

The "Steen", National Maritime Musem.
A room with the history of navigation from the beginning of the 19th century

The "Steen", National Maritime Museum. Small-scale model of the ceremonial barge which brought the Emperor Napoleon to Antwerp in 1810

The "Steen".
courtyart in front
of the entrance

A room in the Maritime Museum with a threemasted galiot (18th century)

Monument at the Noorderterras, remembering the Liberation (1944)

The armed merchantman " Barbersteyn" (1746), a ship of the Dutch East Indian Compagny

The harbour of Antwerp, which extends to the Dutch
frontier, covers an area of 14.000 ha.
(Foto:Guido Coolens)

A harbour trip by a "Flandria" boat
normally takes 3 hours

As far as possible, the emphasis is educational. We
can learn much about the customs of seamen, life on
the waterfront, superstition and devotion, internal
navigation, cartography, the art of navigation and the
building and development of the ship. Finally there is
a review of Belgian maritime history.

Near to the Steen, by the floating bridge, is the landing
stage of the "Flandria" ships. This shipping company

View of the harbour entrance : the Zandvliet lock and the Berendrecht lock, which is the largest in the world.
(Foto:Guido Coolens)

offers a wide selection of excursions by boat, beginning with a trip on the river Scheldt or a trip round the harbour lasting three hours, and extending to day excursions along the Belgian coast or to Vlissingen and Rotterdam.

The trip round the harbour gives a good impression of the intense activity there and is especially interesting. It is possible to explore the harbour by private car; the City Tourist Office has produced a Harbour Route map covering some 80 km and extending to the Dutch border.

A view at the quays of the Delwaide dock, the Canal docks, the river Scheldt and the Nuclear Power Station at Doel.

(Foto:Guido Coolens)

The floating crane "Brabo" (liftcapacity: 800 Ton)

(Foto:Guido Coolens)

The Open-Air Museum of Sculpture " Middelheim". Statue by Rik Wouters " Household cares".

The Open-Air Museum of Sculpture " Middelheim" near the "Nachtegalenpark" enjoys world-wide renown. Ist was founded through the initiative of Burgomaster Lode Craeybeckx in 1950.

The park is accessible by public transport from Groenplaats or Koningin Astridplein. Private cars take the Brussels road.

The collection represents modern sculpture from August Rodin to the present day. By regularly purchasing contemporary works the museum ensures that it represents the evolution of modern sculpture. Every second year there is an international "Biënnale" which gives sculptors from a specific country or group of countries the chance to exhibit their most modern creations.

The "Middelheim Park" together with "Vogelenzang" and "Den Brandt" form the "Nachtegalenpark", covering 80 ha. The "Hortiflora"-Garden in the "Vogelenzang" Park at the side of Beukenlaan opposite "Den Brandt" provides a restful interval.

Vic Gentils. "Burgomaster Lode Craeybeckx"

George Grard. "Niobe"

Max Bill. "Unending twist"

Constant Permeke. "Mary Lou"

Antwerp, "A City on the River". A city, that thanks to the river Scheldt, feels in touch with the whole world. (Foto:Guido Coolens)

A view at the Town Hall and the renovated old city centre ➡

Antwerp, a "City on the River", is a city that feels itself part of the whole world, on account of the river Scheldt. It is a city that offers a wealth of cultural and historical interest, as your walks and museum visits have shown, and also a city of culinary interest. Cafés and restaurants are concentrated in the old city centre around the Grote Markt and the Cathedral and in the vicinity of Central Station.

There is no shortage of comfortable places on terraces or in cafés and restaurants. The top restaurants provide gastronomic delights that make a lunch break or an evening out into a feast. But for those who are content with simpler fare, there is also a wide choise. As far as regional gastronomy is concerned, Antwerp must hold its own with other towns and localities. We should first mention mussels, which are prepared in various ways: the normal way of cooking with onion, celery and herbs, served in the pot with some mustard sauce is the best way. "Paling in 't groen" (eel in a green sauce) is a delicacy that is served hot or cold. These are only two examples of the extensive array of dishes that most restaurants offer.

Antwerp at night near the Central Station

*Another popular street near the
Suikerrui and the cathedral*

As you could expect in a port, there are may foreign restaurants, especially around the Central Station and the harbour, which offer inexpensive and excellent food. Troughout the city there are the stalls, where at reasonable cost you can buy ships and sausage. A portion of chips is a good idea, if you get hungry on a walk

The numerous café terraces and inns are an invitation to become familiar with the art of beer drinking. Belgium is known worldwide for its beer consumption and Antwerp gives a lead. Each kind of beer is served in its special

The Grote Markt provides a place where residents and tourists can meet throughout the day and late into the night

The courtyard of "De Gulden Handt", which was once the salt exchange , but is now a Spanish wine dealer

glass and the choice is great. Inns with more than 20 kinds of beer are common and there are some places that offer more than 500 varieties.

"Antwerpse handjes" are biscuits or chocolates in the shape a of a hand and they originate in the Brabo-legend. They can be obtained in most bakers and confectioners. The exquisite pralines made from fine Belgian chocolate will delight your palate; they are an ideal gift with which to treat family and friends.

Whoever wants to make purchases or to find souvenirs will head for the busy shopping streets. There are also weekly markets of which the most famous is the "Vogel-markt", situated near the Municipal Theatre (Stads-schouwburg) and close to the Rubens House. There are

Rubensmarkt during the week of the Antwerp fairon the Grote Markt

Gallery "Petro Paulo Rubens" on the Groenplaats

The weekly "Vogelmarkt" near the Municipal Theatre

also Antique Markets (on the Lijnwaadmarkt near the Cathedral) and twice a week a "Fridaymarket" for second hand goods.

Folklore Markets are also held on the Grote Markt and on St.Jansplein. The most crowded is the "Rubensmarkt" on August 15th during the week of the Antwerp Fair.

There is a long tradition of fairs in Antwerp. Throughout the year there is something on. Early in the year there is the Carnival Procession; in the former southern docks, there is the Sinksenfoor and during the Antwerp Fair there are may festivities where the Rhetorians play an important role. Liberation celebrations are held on the Grote Markt and other festivities, too numerous to mention.

A lace maker near the Groenplaats in the vicinity of the Cathedral

The Provincial Museum "Sterckshof" at Deurne

The castle in the Provincial Domain "Rivierenhof" at Deurne

The castle "Den Brandt" in "Nachtegalenpark"

There is something to do every evening in Antwerp. There are more than 50 cinemas in the city and performances begin in the afternoon. Films are shown in the original version. Moreover Antwerp prides itself on the largest number of theatres and auditoriums. No other place offers more in the way of plays, concerts, opera and ballet.

Anyone desiring a respite from the heart of the city can visit the Left Bank or the villages of the Polder, by public transport or private car.
On the outskirts of the city there are parks and castles together with numerous small but interesting museums. In addition there are green areas for sport and

recreation. Outside the green belt that surrounds the city, there are opportunities for recreation in the "Reigers Wood", a nature reserve at Berendrecht, in "Veltwijck Park" at Ekeren, in "Ter Rivierenhof" and "Boekenbergpark" at Deurne, in the Parks of "Sorghvliet" and "Broydenborg" at Hoboken and other sites too numerous to mention.

There are peaceful footpaths and rides at the St. Anna-Bos on the Left Bank.

Many visitors are attracted to the Polder Region for the "gansrijden" on Carnival Sunday and in the Mid-Lent, where the old custom is preserved in the villages of Berendrecht, Hoevenen, Lillo, Stabroek and Zandvliet. This is a folklore game, today using artificial geese.

A footpath on the Left Bank by the St.Anna Mill

The yacht harbour on the Left Bank

Your expeditions in the city will have shown you that Antwerp is a hospitable place, with a friendly welcome for all who come from near or far.

The walks suggested in the book, linking museums to churches and other places of interest, can naturally not be completed in one day. More time is needed and a day in Antwerp will be a memorable introduction, arousing your appetite to see and experience more. Antwerp is a city to love and whoever comes once will gladly return.

* * * * *

Collection ALL EUROPE

#		Spanish	French	English	German	Italian	Catalan	Dutch	Swedish	Portuguese	Japanese	Finnish
1	ANDORRA	•	•	•	•	•	•					
2	LISBON	•	•	•	•	•				•		
3	LONDON	•	•	•	•	•					•	
4	BRUGES	•	•	•	•	•		•				
5	PARIS	•	•	•	•	•					•	
6	MONACO	•	•	•	•	•						
7	VIENNA	•	•	•	•	•						
11	VERDUN	•	•	•	•			•				
12	THE TOWER OF LONDON	•	•	•								
13	ANTWERP	•	•	•	•	•		•				
14	WESTMINSTER ABBEY	•	•	•								
15	THE SPANISH RIDING SCHOOL IN VIENNA	•	•	•								
16	FATIMA	•	•	•	•	•				•		
17	WINDSOR CASTLE	•	•	•	•	•					•	
19	COTE D'AZUR	•	•	•	•	•						
22	BRUSSELS	•	•	•	•	•		•				
23	SCHÖNBRUNN PALACE	•	•	•	•	•		•				
24	ROUTE OF PORT WINE	•	•	•	•	•				•		
26	HOFBURG PALACE	•	•	•	•	•						
27	ALSACE	•	•	•	•	•		•				
31	MALTA			•	•	•						
32	PERPIGNAN		•									
33	STRASBOURG	•	•	•	•	•						
34	MADEIRA + PORTO SANTO		•	•	•					•		
35	CERDAGNE - CAPCIR		•			•						
36	BERLIN	•	•	•	•	•						

Collection ART IN SPAIN

#		Spanish	French	English	German	Italian	Catalan	Dutch	Swedish	Portuguese	Japanese	Finnish
1	PALAU DE LA MUSICA CATALANA	•		•		•						
2	GAUDI	•	•	•	•	•					•	
3	PRADO MUSEUM I (Spanish Painting)	•	•	•	•	•					•	
4	PRADO MUSEUM II (Foreign Painting)	•	•	•	•	•						
5	MONASTERY OF GUADALUPE	•										
6	THE CASTLE OF XAVIER	•	•	•	•						•	
7	THE FINE ARTS MUSEUM OF SEVILLE	•	•	•	•	•						
8	SPANISH CASTLES	•	•	•	•							
9	THE CATHEDRALS OF SPAIN	•	•	•	•							
10	THE CATHEDRAL OF GERONA	•	•	•	•							
14	PICASSO	•	•	•	•	•					•	
15	REALES ALCAZARES (ROYAL PALACE OF SEVILLE)	•	•	•	•	•						
16	MADRID'S ROYAL PALACE	•	•	•	•	•						
17	ROYAL MONASTERY OF EL ESCORIAL	•	•	•	•	•						
18	THE WINES OF CATALONIA	•										
19	THE ALHAMBRA AND THE GENERALIFE	•	•	•	•	•						
20	GRANADA AND THE ALHAMBRA	•										
21	ROYAL ESTATE OF ARANJUEZ	•	•	•	•							
22	ROYAL ESTATE OF EL PARDO	•	•	•	•							
23	ROYAL HOUSES	•	•	•	•	•						
24	ROYAL PALACE OF SAN ILDEFONSO	•	•	•	•							
25	HOLY CROSS OF THE VALLE DE LOS CAIDOS	•	•	•	•	•						
26	OUR LADY OF THE PILLAR OF SARAGOSSA	•	•	•		•						
27	TEMPLE DE LA SAGRADA FAMILIA	•	•	•	•	•	•					
28	POBLET ABTEI	•	•	•	•			•				

Collection ALL SPAIN

#		Spanish	French	English	German	Italian	Catalan	Dutch	Swedish	Portuguese	Japanese	Finnish
1	ALL MADRID	•	•	•	•	•					•	
2	ALL BARCELONA	•	•	•	•	•	•					
3	ALL SEVILLE	•	•	•	•	•					•	
4	ALL MAJORCA	•	•	•	•	•						
5	ALL THE COSTA BRAVA	•	•	•	•	•						
6	ALL MALAGA and the Costa del Sol	•	•	•	•	•			•			
7	ALL THE CANARY ISLANDS (Gran Canaria)	•	•	•	•	•				•	•	
8	ALL CORDOBA	•	•	•	•	•					•	
9	ALL GRANADA	•	•	•	•	•			•			
10	ALL VALENCIA	•	•	•	•	•						
11	ALL TOLEDO	•	•	•	•	•					•	
12	ALL SANTIAGO	•	•	•	•	•						
13	ALL IBIZA and Formentera	•	•	•	•	•						
14	ALL CADIZ and the Costa de la Luz	•	•	•	•							
15	ALL MONTSERRAT	•	•	•	•	•	•					
16	ALL SANTANDER and Cantabria	•										
17	ALL THE CANARY ISLANDS II, (Tenerife)	•	•	•	•	•			•	•		•
20	ALL BURGOS	•	•	•	•	•						
21	ALL ALICANTE and the Costa Blanca	•	•	•	•	•			•			
22	ALL NAVARRA	•	•	•								
23	ALL LERIDA	•	•	•	•				•			
24	ALL SEGOVIA	•	•	•	•							
25	ALL SARAGOSSA	•	•	•	•	•						
26	ALL SALAMANCA	•	•	•	•	•				•		
27	ALL AVILA	•	•	•	•	•						
28	ALL MINORCA	•	•	•	•	•						
29	ALL SAN SEBASTIAN and Guipúzcoa	•										
30	ALL ASTURIAS	•		•								
31	ALL LA CORUNNA and the Rías Altas	•	•	•	•							
32	ALL TARRAGONA	•	•	•	•	•						
33	ALL MURCIA	•	•	•								
34	ALL VALLADOLID	•	•	•								
35	ALL GIRONA	•	•	•								
36	ALL HUESCA	•	•									
37	ALL JAEN	•	•	•								
38	ALL ALMERIA	•	•	•								
40	ALL CUENCA	•	•	•								
41	ALL LEON	•	•	•								
42	ALL PONTEVEDRA, VIGO and the Rías Bajas	•	•	•								
43	ALL RONDA	•	•	•	•	•						
44	ALL SORIA	•										
46	ALL EXTREMADURA	•										
47	ALL ANDALUSIA	•	•	•	•							
52	ALL MORELLA	•	•		•							

Collection ALL AMERICA

#		Spanish	French	English	German	Italian	Catalan	Dutch	Swedish	Portuguese	Japanese	Finnish
1	PUERTO RICO	•		•								
2	SANTO DOMINGO	•		•								
3	QUEBEC			•	•							
4	COSTA RICA	•		•								
5	CARACAS	•		•								

Collection ALL AFRICA

#		Spanish	French	English	German	Italian	Catalan	Dutch	Swedish	Portuguese	Japanese	Finnish
1	MOROCCO	•	•	•	•	•						
2	THE SOUTH OF MOROCCO	•	•	•	•	•						
3	TUNISIA		•	•	•	•						
4	RWANDA		•									